A Child's First Book

of Jewish Holidays

Alfred J. Kolatch

Illustrated by
Harry Araten

JD | JONATHAN DAVID PUBLISHERS, INC.
Middle Village, New York 11379

A CHILD'S FIRST BOOK OF JEWISH HOLIDAYS

Jonathan David Publishers, Inc.
68-22 Eliot Avenue
Middle Village, New York 11379

4 6 8 10 9 7 5

Library of Congress Cataloging-in-Publication Data

Kolatch, Alfred J.
    A child's first book of jewish holidays / Alfred J. Kolatch illustrated by Harry Araten.
        p. cm.
    Summary: Introduces Jewish days of celebration including Shabbat, Rosh Hashana, Yom Kippur, Sukkot, Simchat Torah, Chanukah, Tu Bi-Shevat, Purim, Passover, Lag B'omer, Shavuot, Tisha B'av, and Yom Ha-Atzmaut
    ISBN 0-8246-0393-1
    1. Fasts and feasts—Judaism—Juvenile literature. [1. Fasts and feasts—judaism. 2. Judaica—customs and practices.] I. Araten.
BM690.K634 1997   97-11945
296.4'3—dc21   CIP
                                                               AC r97

Designed and composed by John Reinhardt Book Design

Printed in China

For Meghan, Erin, and Jonathan

A.J.K.

For Rachel and our three children

Devra, Yaël, and Gideon

H.A.

Contents

Shabbat

On Friday night Mommy lights the Shabbat candles and Daddy makes *Kiddush.*

8

On Saturday night,
when three stars
appear in the sky,
we make *havdala*
and welcome in
the new week.

Rosh Hashana

This is a *shofar*.
When I am older,
I will learn how
to blow it on
Rosh Hashana.

After we pray in the synagogue,
we wish everyone "Happy New Year!"
At home we dip apple in honey for a sweet New Year.

Yom Kippur

On Yom Kippur
my family spends
the whole day
in the synagogue.

Mommy and Daddy do not eat or drink.

They pray for good health and peace.

13

Sukkot

We are building a *sukka* in our backyard.

Mommy and Daddy say a special prayer while holding the *lulav* and *etrog*.

15

Simchat Torah

This is our Torah. We hug it and kiss it on Simchat Torah.

We form a circle and dance round and round holding the Torah.

Chanuka

Chanuka is my favorite holiday. I receive many gifts.

I light my *menora*,
and Daddy
lights the
big *menora*.

מְעַנוֹג צְדִיק יְשׁוּעָתִי

We all sing happy songs and eat delicious potato latkes.

I love to spin the *draydel*.
When it falls on the
letter *gimmel*, I win!

21

Tu Bi-Shevat

Winter is over.
Springtime has
come to Israel.

22

Buds are on every tree. Tu Bi-Shevat is here!

Purim

On Purim we read the Megilla.

It tells the story of
Mordecai and Esther.

When wicked Haman's name is read, I turn my grogger and stamp my feet.

Passover

Passover is a family time.

Everyone comes to my house to celebrate the *Seder*.

We eat *matza* and drink wine.

If I find the *afikomon*,
I get a prize.

Lag B'Omer

In the month of May, we celebrate Lag B'Omer day.
The children in Israel go on picnics,
roast marshmallows, and shoot arrows into the air.

Shavuot

On Shavuot
Moses went up to the
top of Mount Sinai.

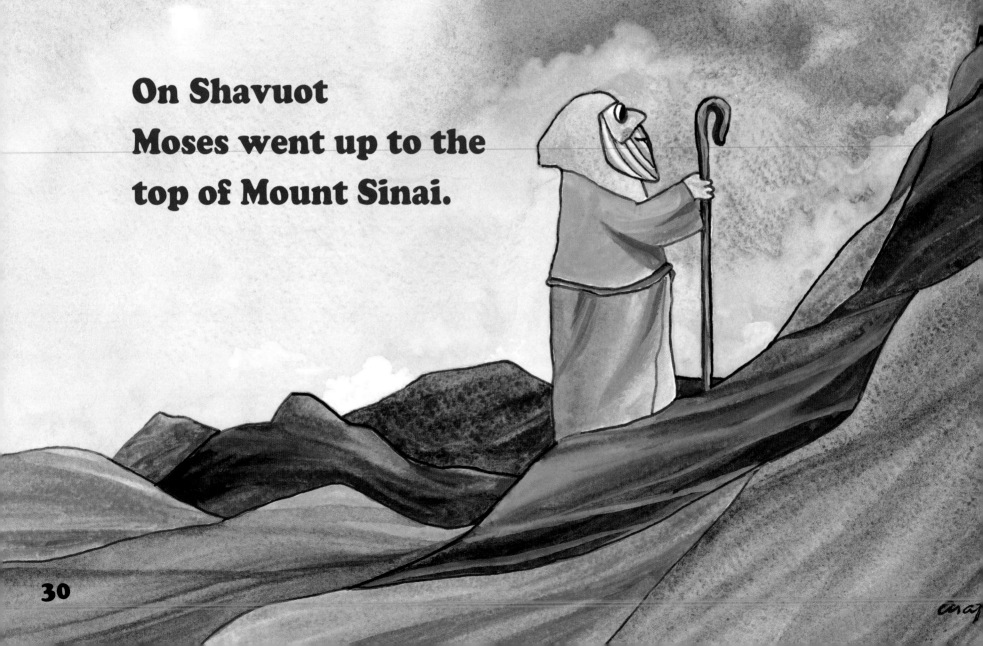

There, God gave him
the Ten Commandments.

Tisha B'Av

Tisha B'Av is the ninth day of Av.

On this day
a long time ago,
the Temple in Jerusalem
was burned to the ground.

Yom Ha-Atzma'ut

I am waving the Israeli flag to celebrate Yom Ha-Atzma'ut.

On this day Israel was born.
Happy Birthday, Israel!